Haiku in English

Haiku in English

by Harold G. Henderson

CHARLES E. TUTTLE COMPANY
Rutland, Vermont & Tokyo, Japan

Published by the Charles E. Tuttle Company, Inc.
of Rutland, Vermont & Tokyo, Japan
with editorial offices
at Suido 1-chome, 2-6, Bunkyo-ku, Tokyo

Library of Congress Catalog Card No. 67-16413
International Standard Book No. 0-8048-0228-9

First printing, 1967
Twenty-third printing, 1990

PRINTED IN JAPAN

I wish to express my thanks for the generous cooperation of all those who have assisted in preparing this discussion of the problems involved in writing haiku in English, most of whom are mentioned in the text. I wish particularly to acknowledge my indebtedness to the staff of the Japan Society for its continued encouragement and support and especially to Mr. Daniel Meloy whose untiring assistance has been invaluable.

HAROLD G. HENDERSON

Table of Contents

Publisher's Foreword

HAIKU, in recent years, has gained a worldwide popularity that has both pleased and displeased the purists of the art in the country where it has been in existence for centuries. Many of them believe that one *must* be Japanese to experience the full impact and emotion to be gleaned from the abbreviated form of poetry. Others are happy and appreciate the attempt by Westerners to understand and therefore become enriched by the explosive simplicity which haiku is meant to impart.

The non-Japanese speaking world has had only translations by which to expose themselves to this art. While being a far cry from the originals, they have been sufficient to ignite the spark that has made haiku current.

Its concise nature has given many to the belief that haiku is not a difficult form of poetry—neither to read and understand nor to write. The result has been thousands of mechanically produced 17-syllable poems that can be called haiku with the same effect that one might get in comparing a giant sequoia to bonsai.

To assist those who are interested in finding out more about haiku before they undertake to create

9

their own compositions, we are proud to be able to offer this introductory booklet with an eye to providing greater understanding to the large numbers who have given it the enthused attention it has received in the last several years.

Haiku in English was originally published by the Japan Society of New York, a group with the purpose of bringing "the people of the United States and Japan closer together in their appreciation and understanding of each other and each other's way of life." Our cooperation with the Society which enables us to give this work a wider circulation is another step toward fulfilling our goal of providing "Books to Span the East and West."

Introductory Note

Haiku is a form of poetry which Japanese have practiced for centuries, and which, literally, millions of Japanese are writing today. In the last ten years or so it has become popular in America. First hundreds, then thousands, now many tens of thousands of Americans are writing haiku—or at least trying to.

The Japan Society has received numerous requests for information about how to write haiku in English. We do not feel that we can give any complete or even adequate answer to this question. Nevertheless, it may be possible to propose certain guide lines, and suggest certain ideas, which could be of help to those who wish to produce haiku in English.

It seems to us that the problem may well be divided into three parts:

1. What is a Japanese haiku?

2. What is, or should be, a haiku in English?

3. What should an English-speaking person do in order to write (or teach) haiku in English?

Japanese Haiku

The ideal first step in learning just what a Japanese haiku really is, would be, of course, to read a great many in the original Japanese. This, however, is not possible for most Americans, and the only substitute is to read them in translations.

Unfortunately, no translation of a poem is ever *absolutely* faithful to the original, and many so-called translations of haiku have been very unfaithful indeed. For the serious student we recommend R. H. Blyth's monumental *Haiku* in 4 volumes, and especially his recently published *History of Haiku* in 2 volumes (Tokyo, Hokuseido Press, 1964). These books give the original Japanese as well as translations, and almost every haiku is discussed separately. We also recommend H. G. Henderson's *An Introduction to Haiku* (New York, Doubleday and Co., Inc., 1958, also in paperback). This is a far less comprehensive work than Blyth's, but has the advantage of footnotes which give both the originals and word for word translations. Another useful book is Kenneth Yasuda's *Japanese Haiku* (Rutland, Vermont, Charles E. Tuttle Co., Inc., 1957) even though it does not give the Japanese originals.

For those who cannot go back to the originals we

13

offer the following analysis of the external characteristics of classical Japanese haiku stet.

As a general rule a classical Japanese haiku:

1. consists of 17 Japanese syllables (5–7–5)

2. contains at least some reference to nature (other than human nature)

3. refers to a particular event (i.e., it is not a generalization)

4. presents that event as happening *now*—not in the past.

None of these "general rules" is followed a full 100% of the time although very nearly so. The one most frequently broken is rule 1. The small number of exceptions to the other rules are usually more apparent than real.

"Rule" 1

Japanese haiku "syllables" used for the 5–7–5 count are not English syllables. They are rather units of duration. Every Japanese syllable either is a short vowel or ends with one. Each is represented by its own *kana* symbol or "character" and is counted as one unit. A nasal "n" sound has a special *kana*

symbol and also counts as one unit. A long vowel is written with 2 characters and is counted as 2 units. E.g., *Onjôji* (O-n-jo-o-ji) is counted as 5 units. Furthermore, a doubled consonant, which automatically entails a pause (as in the English "rat-tail"), is counted as an extra unit. E.g., *Nippon* (Ni-p-po-n) would count as 4 units. It is worth noting that the Japanese word *ji-on*—usually translated as "syllable" —literally means "character-sound."

About one haiku in 25 does not have a strict 5–7–5 form. The variation from the rule, however, is usually not more than one syllable. An example is the famous early haiku by Teishitsu (1609–73), which is in 6–7–5 form:

Kore wa kore wa to bakari hana no Yoshinoyama

> Oh . . . ! that's all
> upon the blossomed-covered
> hills of Yoshino.

(The translation is as literal as possible, except for the word "upon." This has been added, for English-speaking readers, to bring out that the poet actually is on the mountain, and trying to compose a poem about it. *Kore wa kore wa* is all he can say, or write.)

"Rule" 2

The reference to nature is not always direct. Classical haiku almost all contain so-called "season-words" which may be connected with a particular season only by convention. Their use is considered a reference to nature even if it is not a reference to particular natural objects, such as snow or cherry-blossoms. A mention of "piercing cold" sets the season as late autumn; of "a bell ringing clearly" as winter; "New Year's Day" (which usually fell in February) marks the start of spring, etc. The use of season-words like these fully meets the requriements of rule 2 and for centuries it has been the custom to arrange a haiku-poet's work according to the four seasons.

In a haiku like Bashô's:

Ie wa mina tsue ni shiraga no haka mairi

> A family—all
> leaning on staves and white-haired—
> visiting the graves.

the season-word is "visiting the graves," as the traditional season for this is mid-summer. For a reader unfamiliar with season words there is still, however, the implication that not only individuals, and families, must die, but also that all things die, and therefore a tie-up with nature.

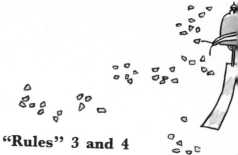

"Rules" 3 and 4

Both these rules (3, one event; 4, happening *now*)—
though they are quite as universal as rules 1 and 2 —
are connected with technique. An apparent exception to these rules is a poem like this, by Onitsura
(1660–1738):

Saku kara ni miru kara ni hana no chiru kara ni

(literally)   Blooming after at
                    viewing after at, blossoms
                        falling after at . . . .

which may be translated as:

The blossom and then
we gaze, and then the bloom
scatters, and then . . . .

It is actually, however, neither a generalization, nor
in the past. It simply shows Onitsura's reaction at the
time when the cherry-bloom is scattering. Indeed, the
last *kara ni* is more nearly equal to "and now. . . ."

These characteristics or general rules indicate that
classical haiku are poems which were, in practice,
restricted in form, in subject, and in technique. However, they do not in themselves constitute a definition
of haiku.

17

Some Developments from these Restrictions

Shortness resulted in the omission of all unnecessary words, and great reliance on suggestion. Many haiku contain no verb at all, and sentences are usually left unfinished. Such omissions encouraged the use of conventional *kireji* (cutting-words), such as *kana* or *ya,* which mark either the end of a haiku or divisions in it. (The study of these *kireji* is interesting, but cannot be gone into here.)

The limitation in length also resulted in the use of certain special techniques, which became accepted as haiku conventions. Perhaps the most important is what may be called the principle of internal comparison. It was first exemplified in a poem by Bashô (1644–94), who is known as "The First Pillar of Haiku":

Kare eda ni karasu no tomarikeri aki no kure

On a withered branch
a crow has settled . . .
autumn nightfall.

The picture is one whole, but the parts are to be compared. There is a suggestion of late autumn, of nightfall settling over a desolate landscape, the contrast of the small black spot with the vast amorphous

darkness, their gradual merging as nightfall becomes night, etc., etc. This is known as a model poem, in spite of the unusual 5–9–5 form. It was, however, written before Bashô had become thoroughly imbued with Zen, and hence is a model for technique only, and not for what came to be known as the Bashô type of haiku.

This comparison technique is not always used, but the reader must be on the lookout for it. The following is a famous Bashô-type haiku by his pupil Ransetsu (1653–1708):

Ume ichi rin ichi rin hodo no atatakasa

(literally)   Plum-tree one blossom
             one blossom extent-up-to
             warmth.

or, changing the order, "warmth to the amount of one blossom."

This does not mean "as the plums bloom it grows warmer"—or even vice-versa. Neither is it a "which came first, chicken-or-egg?" problem. Both the blossom and the "blossom-worth" of warmth exist. As one compares them, more come, and more. Winter is turning into spring, and there is no reasoning about cause and effect.

Buson, the "Second Pillar of Haiku" (1715–83), unlike Bashô, was a famous painter, a man of the world, and as a poet a brilliant technician who carried both the omission of words and the principle of comparison to perhaps their ultimate extent. As an example:

Yadokase to katana nagedasu fubuki kana

(literally) "Night's lodging!" thus
     throwing a sword down
      wind-blown snow . . . .

In the Japanese the *to* (a reflective "that" or "thus") is sufficient to show that a night's lodging is being demanded. To a trained haiku-reader the first picture is that of an exhausted samurai, presumably desperate, storming into a house at night, with snow blowing in through the opened door behind him. But by the principal of comparison the fugitive is compared to "wind-blown snow"—and the snow to him. It is quite possible that the similarity of the sweep of wind-blown snow to the trajectory of a thrown sword was what inspired Buson to compose this haiku.

The reference to nature may be of any kind. At one extreme is a simple description of some natural

thing or event, like

Ochiba ochi kasanarite ame ame wo utsu

> The falling leaves
> fall and pile up; the rain
> beats on the rain. (Gyôdai, 1732–93)

At the other extreme is what may be called an anthropomorphic use of season-words. Examples of such use are Buson's reference to the "piercing cold" in his

Mi ni shimu ya naki tsuma no kushi neya ni fumu

> This piercing cold I feel
> my dead wife's comb, in our bedroom
> under my heel . . . .

or, in another poem, his reminder, to a young lady who won't answer his missives, that springtime is nearly over.

Even in these last two examples, the fact that the season is set adds to the depths of the haiku.

Rules 3 and 4, taken together, suggest that haiku may be regarded as a special way of conveying to the reader the emotions felt by the poet at some particular event. The suggestion is strengthened by a fifth general rule or restriction—not quite so universal as

the first four—that the emotion is conveyed not by stating or describing it, but by describing or clearly suggesting the circumstances that aroused it.

One apparent exception is the use of the common Japanese "emotion-word" *aware,* for which there is no exact English equivalent. It has been translated as "the touchingness of things," and indeed does represent an emotion-raising quality rather than an emotion. For example, Shiki's (1867–1902):

Hito ni nite tsuki yo no kagashi aware nari

may be translated as:

> Being like a man,
> in the moonlit night the scarecrow
> is very touching.

But even here the description of the circumstances is dominant.

The Objectives of Haiku Techniques

From a basic point of view, any poem must convey an emotion. As a classical haiku is connected (a) with some particular event, and (b) with some aspect of nature other than purely human, it may be described as "a record of a moment of emotion in which human nature is somehow linked to all nature."

22

The main objective of all haiku techniques is to recreate the circumstances that aroused the poet's emotion. By putting himself in the same circumstances the reader may experience the emotion directly. Of course, co-operation is required. The reader must consciously try to put himself in the poet's place—see what he sees, hear what he hears, etc., and so feel what he feels. This is one of the reasons why haiku-reading has been called an art in itself.

There is another quality that is common to all haiku even when any one of the so-called general rules is not followed. It may be called a quality of growth—an ability to convey more emotion than is experienced at a first reading. This quality is obvious in those haiku that use the technique of internal comparison, but it can be found in even the simplest haiku.

If the poet's emotion is a simple one, as in Gyôdai's "The falling leaves / fall and pile up; the rain / beats on the rain," not much repetition is needed. But even here repetition deepens the emotion. (The word repetition is used because haiku are so short that re-reading is seldom necessary.)

On the other hand, if the emotion is deep, or complicated, or a mixture of emotions, much repetition is needed. As an example, Bashô's

Matsutake ya shiranu ko-no-ha-no hebaritsuku

> The mushroom:
> > from an unknown tree a leaf
> > sticks to it.

Here the full picture can be gotten at first sight, but the reverberations, especially from the word "unknown" are multifarious.

Even in an early and undeveloped haiku like Teishitsu's verse about the cherry-blossoms at Yoshino, the whole emotion does not come out at the first reading. It is not simply an expression of admiration. It is also the rueful apology of a court poet at his inability to produce the poem expected of him. The reader gets more out of the poem by putting himself in the poet's two positions.

It does not seem necessary, even if it were possible, to discuss the values of classical haiku here. The value of the form and technique seems to be chiefly that they have proved useful in conveying the poet's emotions with great directness and immediacy. The value of any poem depends on the value of what the poet has to convey.

A discussion of haiku values from a Japanese point of view is given in *Haikai and Haiku* (Tokyo, Nippon Gakujutsu Shinkôkai, 1958). Among much other

useful information about *yûgen, sabi, wabi,* etc., not necessarily directly connected with haiku, it points out the difference between what may be called the Bashô and Buson schools of haiku. It notes that in his theories about haiku, "Buson never mentions, as Bashô did, the union of the individual with Nature, but advocates rather exploring and enjoying to the full the world of imagination, irrespective of any philosophy of Nature."

As the distinction is important it seems wise to quote the following from an article by Dr. Tadao Ichiki of Shiga University:

Buson's attitude in composing haiku was quite different from that of Bashô. Bashô's life and art have been said to be one. Haiku was his religion. In order to compose creative haiku he longed to forget himself and to live in that world where Nature and self become one. For Buson, however, life and art were not one. Even though he often forgot the worries of his daily life when he was composing haiku, his attitude towards art was intellectual, aesthetic, and of the art-for-art's sake school. While Bashô composed many high-spirited subjective haiku through which he expressed his insight of life, Buson romantically and objectively described the beauty of the world, classical, legendary and lyrical. And most of his haiku have sensuous beauty which appeals to the visual or auditory sense.

Both types of haiku (sometimes called, though not wholly correctly, the nature-oriented and the human-oriented) have their own values. They are not quite the same. Yet it may, perhaps, be stated without fear of contradiction that any classical haiku, by any poet, shows some awareness of nature; and many are records of moments of special awareness and insight.

It seems impossible to make any definitive statement about the intent of classical haiku in general. Bashô, Buson, Issa, Shiki, et al., each had his own intent. There are, however, two points that should be stressed.

First, the reference to nature is an integral part of a haiku. Even in Buson's: *Mi ni shimu ya naki tsuma no kushi neya ni fumu* (p. 21) the "piercing cold" (literally "it pierces into the body") suggests first the sudden chill of late autumn. The internal cold is compared to it, as well as added on to it, and both the mental and physical cold are integral parts of the haiku.

This, like many human-oriented haiku, can hardly be called a poem primarily about nature. It does, however, seem safe to say that one intent of all classical haiku-poets was to make nature, or some aspect of nature, an integral part of their poems.

The second point has to do with what Yasuda calls "the firm prohibition on overt expressions of

feeling or of argument—the need for sheer statement alone." This is, of course, concerned with technique and has been mentioned in p. 21. It does, however, emphasize that one conscious intent of the poets was to allow the reader to experience his own emotion as directly as possible.

Most classical haiku are in fact, objective description of the circumstances that aroused the poet's emotion in the first place. But even in so-called subjective haiku like Yasui's (1657–1743):

Mugi kuishi kari to omoedo wakare kana

> Wild geese! I know
> that they did eat the barley;
> but when they go . . . .

the emotion is suggested, not described.

The above short analysis of classical Japanese haiku is of course very incomplete. It is presented only as a minimum necessary for the following consideration of haiku in English.

Haiku in English

Haiku—and attempts at haiku—are now (1965) being written in English by the hundred thousand. In the 1964 Japan Air Lines National Haiku Contest 41,000 were submitted. Other thousands are constantly being printed in newspapers, school and college publications, "little" magazines, etc. One publication devoted entirely to haiku (*American Haiku,* P.O. Box 73, Platteville, Wisconsin) is now in its third year and going strong, and volumes of haiku by individual poets are beginning to appear.

All these are encouraging signs. But it is nevertheless true that "haiku in English" is still in its infancy. There are as yet no generally accepted criteria for what haiku in English are, or should be. What kind of poems they will eventually turn out to be will depend primarily on the poets who write them. It seems obvious that they cannot be exactly the same as Japanese haiku—if only because of the difference in language. At the same time, they cannot differ *too* much and still be haiku.

It is true that in this century some Japanese poets have revolted against the old standards for classical haiku, claiming that they were too restrictive, particularly in regard to form and season-words. But

these poets knew what they revolted against, and presumably had their own good reasons for doing so. It would seem that the same should be true of American poets. There is no law compelling them to follow classical Japanese standards for haiku. It does however seem unwise to abandon these standards without knowing anything about them—as some American poets apparently have done.

We therefore present the following analysis of American haiku, with a particular emphasis on how they do, must, or perhaps should differ from classical Japanese haiku. It is presented simply as a guide line. The final decision rests with the poets themselves.

Form

It seems impossible to use the Japanese "syllable" or "duration-unit" count in English, if only because of the concatenation of consonants that often occur at the end of many English syllables. We *could,* as the Japanese do, count "ran" as 2 units (ra-n); "rain" might be 3. But what would be the Japanese count for a word like "wrenched"? The strict Japanese count is simply inapplicable to English.

The question of what form (if any) should be used

in English haiku is still unsettled. Some idea of what American poets are doing can be gotten by considering the haiku that won first prizes in the *American Haiku* and Japan Air Lines contests.

Searching on the wind,
    the hawk's cry
        is the shape of its beak.   (J. W. Hackett)
                                                        1963

Lily:
    out of the water . . .
        out of itself.   (N. Virgilio)
                                                        1963

Sunset: carrying
    a red balloon, he looks back . . .
        a child leaves the zoo.   (W. F. O'Rourke)
                                                        1964

The town clock's face
    adds another shade of yellow
        to the afterglow.   (N. Virgilio)
                                                        1964

The old rooster crows—
    out of the mist come the rocks
        and the twisted pine.   (O. M. B. Southard)
                                                        1965

A bitter morning:
Sparrows sitting together
Without any necks.

(J. W. Hackett)
1964
Japan Air Lines

There is a growing tendency to approximate a 5–7–5 syllable form, but so far no experienced poet or editor has advocated an absolutely strict adherence to it. In the Japan Air Lines contest, 13 of the 100 published (as the best of 41,000 submitted) are not in the 5–7–5 form. The 1963 *American Haiku* has a somewhat larger variation in its published poems; the 1964 *American Haiku* considerably less.

It may safely be said that most American writers of haiku today do use at least an approximation to a 5–7–5 syllable count. But they also employ the devices of stress and rhythm, traditional in English poetry. Few, if any, have an absolutely fixed pattern of rhythm. They do, however, insist that their poems must "sound right." To paraphrase Pope, "some huge stones, vast, white . . ." moves far more slowly than "a little pebble." Both phrases have five syllables but give a quite different effect.

Blyth, in his *History of Haiku,* Vol. II, p. 350, has cited the contrived verse:

In a potato,
Those groans whose forced prayers change nought,
Can never occur.

and he has commented: "This is 5–7–5, but to eye and ear, and to the sense of counting, the 5–7–5 has no meaning whatever."

On the next page he states: "The ideal, that is, the occasionally attainable haiku form in English, would perhaps be three short lines, the second a little longer than the other two; a two-three-two rhythm, but not regularly iambic or anapaestic; rhyme avoided, even if felicitious and accidental."

Many American poets will not agree that Blyth's proposal is the ideal solution, and will continue to write American haiku in whatever form they feel can best convey their emotions. This is as it should be. The 5–7–5 norm of duration-count has proved appropriate for classical Japanese haiku. What form is the best for haiku in English is still an open question. It has, we think, been shown that an invariable 5–7–5 syllable count is not an adequate answer.

Even the necessity for three lines has been questioned and poets who do use three lines have not agreed on what is the most desirable arrangement. In this booklet all quoted haiku are given as they were originally printed.

Another question of form in which haiku written in English cannot possibly follow their classical Japanese prototypes is in the use of conventional *kireji* (cutting-words) such as *ya* and *kana*. These are primarily verbal punctuation marks, for which we have no exact equivalent. *Ya* is often very much like a colon (:), but not always; *kana,* which is usually used to end a haiku, is often very much like a row of dots (. . . .), but not always. Neither do we have the Japanese "sentence-ending" forms, but of course a period can always be used if desired.

On the whole, American poets do not seem to have been bothered by having no exact equivalent to *kireji*. They seem to have felt that the English language was flexible enough to provide adequate substitutes.

A few poets prefer to write without using any punctuation marks whatever, with pauses indicated only by the ending of lines; others feel this is an unbearable restriction. The question of who is right (possibly both are) will have to be decided by the poets themselves. It does seem, however, that the resources of the English language should be thoroughly investigated, and used wherever appropriate.

For example, duration could be expressed by a series of dots, and Hackett's "hawk" haiku is in its latest version written as:

> Searching on the wind,
> the hawk's cry . . .
> is the shape of its beak.

A third question of form has to do with rhyme. There is no rhyme in classical Japanese haiku. Indeed there hardly could be. In a language in which every syllable ends in a short vowel or an "n" sound, rhyme would soon become intolerably monotonous. The only question is whether rhyme is or is not appropriate to haiku in English.

At present the consensus seems to be against it. Only one rhymed haiku has won any prize in *American Haiku* (Vol. II, No. 2, 2nd prize):

> Brown mimosa seed
> where blossoms once invited
> hummingbirds to feed.   (Ethel Freeman)

There are, however, those who feel that rhyme is always appropriate, and there are also those who believe that in some haiku it may be useful and in others quite out of place.

As an illustration of the reasons given for the differing opinions, those who are against the use of rhyme claim that it tends to close a poem, and that haiku are open. Some of their opponents agree that this is true, but believe that rhyme is especially useful in haiku that "close inward," like the one above, or like Thomas Rountree's:

> On the weathered shelf
> a self-cleaned cat in autumn
> curls around itself.

All agree that there is danger in rhyme, that it may make a haiku tinkly, or may cause the words to distract the reader from the emotion they are meant to convey.

The arguments on both sides are too numerous, and adhered to too passionately, to be given here. However, in *American Haiku,* Vol. III, No. 1, W. H. Kerr has an excellent article on rhyme in haiku—its use, misuse, and possible substitutes for it.

But these again are questions to which only the poets themselves can possibly give final answers.

Nature

Nature, or some aspect of nature, is an integral part of any classical Japanese haiku. So it is for most American haiku. There is, however, a marked difference between the two in the use of season-words, which is practically universal in classical haiku.

American writers can be divided into those who are against their use, those who are for it, and those (apparently the vast majority) who know nothing whatever about it.

The arguments against the use of season-words are (a) that it is impractical and (b) that it is artificial. We cannot just take over the Japanese season-words, because our seasons, flowers, animals, customs, etc., are very different from theirs. Even if they were not, it seems impossible ever to have a body of American haiku-readers who would be willing to learn, as Japanese readers do, that a reference to "the change of servants" or "the change of clothes" sets the season as summer; that an unqualified mention of deer, the moon, or of "a night of stars" is a season-word for autumn, or that bats and sea slugs indicate winter. It is also unquestionable that an over-dependence on season-words can lead to artificiality. There is certainly something wrong when a Japanese book, purporting to show "How to Write Haiku" can consist of practically nothing but a long list of conventionally acceptable season-words. And artificiality is anathema in haiku.

The proponents of season-words admit all this, but claim that their natural use—where both the word and the season suggested are integral parts of the

poem—can give a special kind of depth to a haiku and at the very least makes the writing of successful haiku easier. Certainly, in such a haiku as Buson's "dead wife's comb," unless *mi ni shimu* (pierces into the body) is taken as a season-word suggesting the chill of autumn, much of the poem's effect is lost. Indeed, by strict standards it would not be a haiku at all.

From a different angle, one may consider also Madeleine F. Bennett's:

> The attic—
> a dusty tricycle.
> My child
> has children of his own.

Clement Hoyt, a former editor of *American Haiku,* discussing the difference between haiku and *senryū* (*American Haiku*, No. 2) has called this a "haiku variant," and has said that here "the tricycle and the heartbreak of all the abandoned (the attic) is the poem's center. The poet is not really in this attic, is in truth if not in fact far away with her child and his children. Besides the tricycle hit her in the heart, not the head." It is, of course, also a haiku because there is at least an implied tie-up with the changes natural to all creation.

One perhaps rather extreme proponent of season-words claims that the lack of one here weakens the poem, and that the suggestion of a season—say Spring—would at least "point it up." (He even goes so far as to say that to him "dusty attic" does imply "Spring-Cleaning"!!) The point he makes is that if Spring (the season of new growth) *were* an integral part of the poem, the accent would be on the children, and the poet's joy in them, in spite of her own "heartbreak" and "autumn loneliness." It is given here, not as an interpretation of the poem, but as an example of the effect that proponents of season-words claim that they can have.

Hoyt, and quite a number of others, have proposed that seasons be suggested in haiku in English, by the whole tone of the poem, rather than by conventional season-words. As an example, he feels that the following, by J. M. Dunsmore:

> Each fugitive wave
> flings free, sprawls, sighs—is sucked back
> to a restless grave.

suggests a bleak November, and, more specifically, either at nightfall or at night.

Whatever the final answer may be, it does seem that the whole problem of seasons and season-words

is a very important one, which has up to the present been too much neglected by poets who wish to write haiku in English. The poets themselves are, of course, the court of last resort, but we can, and do, urge that they give more thought to this problem than has been given in the past.

"Rules" 3 and 4

The classical general rule 3—that haiku convey the emotions aroused by one particular event, and are never generalizations—is followed in most American haiku. There are, however, a quite large number of variations from general rule 4—that the event be presented as now—not in the past.

Some of these variations are apparent rather than real. For example, in James W. Dyer's:

> That dead tree's branches
> I, that clump of weeds, and all
> Flowered that summer.

the verb is in the past tense, but the whole feeling of the poem—the emotion—is now.

In other poems, such as Johanna Gravell's:

> Spring came into my room.
> Black work-worn hands bore gently
> The first blue Iris.

the past tense does not seem to add anything. Good as it is, if the present tense had been used, it would have allowed the reader to put himself in the poet's place more easily.

One last example—a curious coincidence. The third-ranked poem in the Japan Air Lines 1964 contest was D. Martin's:

> Sandpipers chased by sea
> Turned and chased
> The sea back again.

Quite independently—and apparently earlier (it was printed in 1963)—J. W. Hackett had written:

> the fleeing sandpipers
> turn about suddenly
> and chase back the sea.

The reader can decide whether the past or present tense is more effective.

So far nothing has been said of classical techniques that are not quite general rules. The technique of internal comparison seems to be used consicously by only a few American poets. Among these is O. M. B. Southard, who wrote, among many others:

> Now the leaves are still—
> and only the mocking bird
> lets the moonlight through!

and also:

> On a leaf, a leaf
> is casting a green shadow—
> and the tree-frog sings!

There is nothing difficult or esoteric about comparing the song to the moonlight, the green shadow to the green frog, etc. Indeed, it seems utterly natural. The technique is in fact so natural that even school-children use it, often quite unconsciously. Take, for example, the following, by Gay Weiner (Hunter, N. Y. Class 4–1, 1963):

> Gold, brown, and red leaves
> All twirling and scattering
> As the children play.

Young Miss Weiner had not been instructed about technique. She had simply been asked to write a poem, in 5–7–5 form, expressing an emotion "mostly about nature." (It has not been possible to discuss this with her directly, but it seems likely that she saw the relationship between the twirling leaves and the dancing children, but not that between the children and the dying leaves.)

Incidentally, this poem illustrates one point that has been claimed for haiku, namely, that it does not

41

only let the reader experience the poet's emotions, but that, by opening a door, it lets the reader go through it and experience his own emotions.

Much more could be said about "haiku in English," but we believe that enough has been presented to allow the following conclusions to be drawn.

Conclusions

First, there is as yet no complete unanimity among American poets (or editors) as to what constitutes a haiku in English—how it differs from other poems which may be equally short. In other words, haiku in English are still in their infancy.

Second, there is increasing agreement on certain basic points. The vast majority of haiku in English, whatever their form, do treat nature, or some aspect of nature, as an integral part of the poem. Most express an emotion aroused by some one particular event, and try to convey it to the reader as simply as possible.

Third, the majority of American poets do not seem to be familiar with the techniques developed by the Japanese haiku-masters. It is not suggested that these techniques must be adopted, but it does seem obvious that some knowledge of them would be use-

ful, at the very least, as suggestions for developing their own techniques.

The difficulty of deciding just what a haiku in English is, is illustrated in the following examples. This, by Sam Bryan (undoubtedly written with tongue in cheek):

> Egocentrical
> influentiality
> unsymmetrical.

though it was published as a haiku is considered, by almost everybody, non-haiku. (See James E. Bull's "Color in Haiku." *American Haiku,* Vol. II, No. 2.) It is obviously not haiku, not only because it does not follow the haiku rules but also because it does not convey emotion, and hence is not a poem of any kind.

The question becomes more difficult when we have to do with verses that actually are poems, e.g.,

> "I'm here, Dad!" I said,
> answering, waking in joy—
> but he was still dead!

The author, J. M. Dunsmore, titled this "The Young Dreamer" and claims that it is not a haiku, and was

not intended to be one. We agree with him, and not only because nature is not an integral part of the poem—after all, death is a natural phenomenon. It is not haiku because it has the *senyrû* quality—the crack at the end. Powerful as it is, it lacks the haiku quality of growth. No matter how often it is repeated, no further emotion is produced than is obtained by that first great stab.

A final example is:

> Out they go again,
>> the snakes—east, south, west, north.
>>> Hear that drumming—rain!
>>>> (A. R. King)

The opinion of a slight majority seems to be that it is haiku—*if* the reference to forked lightning and thunder is intended and gets across. If it is simply a description of a rain-dance, it is not haiku.

The above judgment leads to one quite interesting conclusion, namely that at least to some extent the development of haiku in English may depend on the existence of a body of trained readers as well as a body of trained writers. This may be an argument against the use of any haiku conventions. Proponents of conventions claim, however, that the first audience

for any writer of haiku in English will be his fellow-poets, and that whatever conventions they accept will probably eventually be accepted by the general reader. True or not, the idea is certainly interesting.

Writing and Teaching Haiku

The following suggestions about how to write haiku in English are necessarily suggestions only. They are a compendium of such opinions—of poets, teachers, editors, etc.—as we have been able to gather together.

They are based on the assumption that haiku in English should, at least in the beginning, conform to the standards of haiku in Japanese as far as is practicable. Complete adherence to Japanese standards is, as has been shown, impossible. However, experience has proved that beginners, unless they know at least something about Japanese standards and conventions, are apt to produce poems that have no relation whatever to haiku except in form.

The above assumption does not mean that we think it desirable that haiku in English should be simply shadows of their Japanese forebears. Indeed, we look forward to the day when writers (and readers) of haiku in English will have their own standards and conventions. These will necessarily be somewhat different from the Japanese. But they cannot be *too* different and the poems still be haiku.

Haiku for Beginners

There seems to be complete agreement among teach-

ers that haiku for beginners, especially school children, should be kept as simple as possible. There is, however, no general agreement about methods, or even about objectives. Some teach haiku as an introduction to poetry in general, or to Japanese culture; others to increase interest in nature or awareness of the world around us; others, of course, teach haiku for their own sake.

Each teacher, of course, has special problems. We cannot attempt to answer them all. We feel, however, that there is much to be said for the proponents of teaching haiku for their own sake, who claim that, if they do this, all else is added unto them.

The most general area of agreement is on form. It is generally taught that the form should be 17 English syllables divided into three lines of 5, 7, and 5. A few modify this by adding "about" or "approximately." Almost all specify that a haiku should be unrhymed.

The advantages, for beginners, of using a strict form are two-fold. First, it makes for simplicity. Second, it is excellent practice, not only for haiku, but for every kind of writing. As one college professor put it: "Before attempting flexibility, learn to submit to controls."

One danger of insisting on a strict 5–7–5 form is

that a beginner may get the idea that form is all-important—that any conglomeration of words in 5–7–5 form *is* a haiku, and that every haiku must have that form exactly. It is a real danger, as this idea is already far too prevalent.

Another danger is that an English verse *can* have a strict 5–7–5 syllable count and still not sound right. However, such verses seem to occur rather rarely in actual practice. When they do, they can usually be quite easily corrected by a competent teacher.

As to the use of rhyme, even its most ardent adherents believe that it should not be required of beginners, that to do so would interfere with the simple, natural use of words so necessary in haiku. They do claim, however, that it should not be ruled out if it occurs normally, naturally, and without striving.

The counterpart of general rule 2 for Japanese haiku—that it contain some reference to nature—is usually given to children in some such form as "a haiku is a poem about nature." This of course is not adequate nor even wholly true, but it has the advantage of simplicity and is not likely to mislead young beginners too much. Certainly the beginning is not the place to introduce them to complicated questions about season-words, etc.

Nevertheless it is necessary to stress the intimate relationship between haiku and nature from the very start. It is recognized by most adult poets, and by most teachers. But counterparts of such a "haiku" as:

> Just five, seven five
> Having emotion and thought
> It makes a Haiku.

still appear far too often in school publications. This of course is not a haiku. It is not even a poem. It is a statement, in rhythmic prose, about haiku. It may be informative, but it conveys no sense of emotion at all.

Each class of course presents special problems, and we can suggest no single formula that will answer them all. We therefore suggest that teachers use their own words to bring out the following points:

a. that a haiku is intimately connected with nature. (In more formal words, that some aspect of nature is an integral part of any haiku—even haiku in English.)

b. that a haiku is not necessarily *wholly* about nature. (Strictly speaking, a haiku is not *about* nature at all. It is rather *about* some moment of human emotion.)

For beginners who are already mature it seems best to elaborate on this last statement. Such a haiku as Issa's (1762–1826):

Tsuyu chiru ya musai kono yo ni yô nashi to

A dewdrop fades away:

> It's dirty, this world, and in it
> there's no place for me.

is an illustration. Issa is not here really writing about an actual dewdrop. He is mourning the death of his baby daughter—his own "dewdrop."

Another example is Bashô's "family visiting the graves" (given on p. 16) in which the season is summer. This makes a background of lush summer foliage, and a contrast to the wintry group of "white-haired" people. The season is therefore an integral part of the poem, but certainly not its subject.

The third general rule for classical haiku (that it has to do with one particular event—or, rather, the emotion arising from it) is of very great importance. It is, however, not as yet thoroughly understood by all writers (and readers) of haiku in English.

Consider, for example, the following, by David Mixner, a pupil in Woodstown High School, N. H (1962):

What would happen if
Ants were tall and people small,
Would they step on us?

In spite of certain technical defects, this would be understood by a reader accustomed to Japanese haiku as referring to one particular event. Presumably the boy had turned over a stone, as most boys have when they had the opportunity, and was watching the ants scurry. It is not clear when, or by whom, the suggestion of stepping on the ants was made. Nevertheless it does represent a boy's moment of awareness (or, as some prefer to call it, "awareness of the moment"), his sense of kinship with other living things, etc. And also, the reader (at least, a trained reader) is enabled to put himself in the boy's position and experience his emotion.

It must be added that one prominent American haiku poet disagrees with the above statement on a technical point. He does not consider it a haiku as it stands, but in answer to a suggestion says that it would "become a haiku if the first line were changed to 'Turning a stone—if'. The immediacy and life of this line does I think redeem the moralizing of the rest." Certainly some such emendation may be necessary for American readers, but in any case the com-

ment does emphasize the fact that every haiku is concerned with one particular event.

The term "one particular event" has proved to be difficult for some beginners, especially children. Some teachers have tied rules 2 and 3 together, and said that haiku are "about something in nature." However inaccurate this phrasing may be, it seems to have been a satisfactory introduction—at least sometimes. Other teachers have simply put a ban on all generalizations. We can offer no suggestions, except to urge the necessity of stressing the idea of one particular event from the very start. The idea is so fundamental in Japanese haiku that we do not believe that any poet attempting to write haiku in English can ignore it and still write haiku.

Practically every practicing poet and experienced teacher agrees that beginners in haiku, of whatever age, should not bother about special techniques, but stick to fundamentals. Their advice boils down to "Be simple, be direct, and above all, be natural."

There is also general agreement that beginners should as soon as possible take their own actual experiences as subjects for their haiku. It has been suggested, for adults, that they make a practice of carrying a note-book, and of jotting down in it memoranda of any experience they wish to preserve, at the very

moment they have that experience. Whether those memoranda take the form of finished haiku apparently depends on the individual. Proponents of this idea claim that it not only preserves the emotions of the moment, but also keeps beginners on the alert to notice things.

For children, the note-book idea seems seldom practicable, at least until they have some idea of what a haiku is. They have to be introduced to haiku, through such examples as the teacher feels are appropriate to their age. Also they have to be given some practice in writing in the haiku form. This is apparently quite often done by having them write on more or less prescribed themes before they start writing haiku of their own.

Frank Ankenbrand, Jr., who teaches senior English at Memorial High School, Haddonfield, N. J., and who is a poet in his own right (*Plum Blossom Scrolls,* Audubon, New Jersey, Windward Press, 1962) has this to say of his own experiences in teaching:

Students of all ages are ardent seekers not only of the familiar but of the unknown. To meet a friend cloaked in mystery is a joy to the student and makes him feel a part of this strange and wonderful world of poetry. The very words, "Orient", "East", and "haiku," coupled with the term syllabic verse, awaken deep-seated desires

to become part of this fabled world. By way of introduction I start the students off with Adelaide Crapsey's cinquains, also syllabic in nature, and borrowed from the older form of haiku. A cinquain goes 2,4,6,8,2: a total of twenty-two syllables. Using as illustrations the originator's famous and much anthologized TRIAD [From *Verse,* published in 1938 by Alfred A. Knopf, Inc.]

> These be
> Three silent things:
> The falling snow . . . the hour
> Before the dawn . . . the mouth of one
> Just dead.

I set them to work or have them work with what I call word clusters . . . taking for example the word apple and asking each student what the word brings to his mind. In this way according to the age of the group the answers are more or less sophisticated. A list written on the blackboard might be:

Adam and Eve	taste	applesauce	games
blossoms	Paris	smell	Thanksgiving
fruit	Johnny	William Tell	Newton
songs	Appleseed	color	Halloween
pie	firewood	cider	autumn

and so on until they empty their heads of associated ideas. Then I ask for a list of words for which they might make similar lists. The words run a wide gamut and come quickly as I place them on the blackboard. The class settles down to work; the great need is to get the mind working and have a flow of associations and ideas drip from the ends

of their pens. It is an easy step from cinquain to haiku . . .
the cinquain with its greater freedom and then the rigid
or tighter restrictions of the haiku. This is preceded by
the reading of many of the classic haiku of Japan . . . I
have been fortunate in having had Japanese students
write and recite haiku to my classes in Japanese. At all
times it is impressed upon the learners that they are
writing in English. A striving for the mystical relationship
between non-related subjects is sought and encouraged.
Either by subject or by naming the season outright the
seasonal feeling is achieved.

For pre-teen-age children, several teachers have
reported considerable success in tying up the idea of
composing haiku with that of drawing pictures and
so developing both close observation and expressive
reaction to it. A number of quite charming picture-
and-haiku books have been received from various
schools, indicating that there is at least some validity
in this approach.

Variations of these two methods of getting children
interested in haiku are the only ones that have been
reported to us. It seems quite probable that there may
be other successful methods. The Japan Society
would be grateful for any further practical suggestions.

The type of haiku generally recommended for
beginners is a simple, straightforward description of

the circumstances which aroused the emotion in the
first place. Little Miss Weiner's "Gold, brown, and
red leaves" (p. 41) is a haiku of this type. So is the
following, by an adult beginner, V. Lie:

> Squatting motionless
>> the sun-tanned child and the toad
>> stare at each other.

In both poems the picture is there, given in just
enough detail to allow the reader to put himself in
the author's position, and so experience the author's
emotion directly.

It seems advisable that all beginners should master
this purely objective type of haiku before going on to
others. It is the easiest for children to learn. Adults
sometimes have more trouble with it than children
do, perhaps because it seems too elementary. But successful writers of haiku in English (Hackett, Virgilio, Southard, et al.) have found that practice in
this type of haiku is useful, not only for its own sake,
but also as an invaluable part of their training.

The simplest type of objective haiku has to do with
an observed relationship between two separate things.
E.g., Bashô's crow and nightfall, mushroom and
leaf; Virgilio's clock-face and afterglow; Hackett's
sandpipers and sea; etc., etc. The relationship does

not, of course, have to be between just two things. It may be between three things, as in Shiki's:

Tsuki ichi-rin hoshi musû sora midori kana

> One full moon,
> stars numberless, the sky
> dark green . . . .

Or it may be between different aspects of the same thing, as in Dunsmore's "wave" haiku. Objective haiku that depend on purely visual impressions are often called "picture" haiku, and are the type favored by, and for, most beginners.

The greatest difficulty all beginners seem to have with picture haiku is that of concentrating on making the picture clear, and omitting their own interpretations. For example, the first draft of Lie's child-toad poem had, as the last line, "stare curiously." "Curiously" is of course an unfortunately vague word, which might mean either "peculiarly" or "with curiosity," but the main point here is that the picture was not completed. The author of course knew that the child and the toad were looking at each other; a reader might guess it, but could not be sure; by introducing her own judgment she made it quite possible for the two to be looking at her.

So many children are attempting to write haiku in English that it is very difficult to make a valid general statement about their efforts. There is, however, one failing so very general that it needs to be noticed. This is the apparently quite widespread habit of ending their efforts with a line like "it makes me feel gay," or "it is beautiful." Such lines violate the prohibition against "overt expression of feeling" but also use space needed to make the picture clear.

It should be noted that we are here speaking of objective haiku only. In other types it is quite possible for the poet to give his own emotions or judgments as an integral part of the haiku. As an example, take the following (by Issa), which may be considered as an answer to a child's question:

Hito wo toru kinoko hatashite utsukushiki

> It kills people,
>   this kind of mushroom—
>   Of course it's pretty!

Objective haiku do not necessarily make use of the sense of sight. Other senses may be used in observing things and events. Thus Buson uses both sight and smell in his

Ume-ga-ka no tachinoborite ya tsuki-no-kasa

> From the plum-tree bloom
>> is fragrance floating upward?
>>> There's a halo round the moon.

Onitsura uses touch and sound in his

Suzukaze ya kôkû in michite matsu no koe

> A cooling breeze—
>> and the whole sky is filled
>>> with pine-tree voices.

Issa, in his

Yûdachi ya hadaka de norishi hadaka-uma

> A sudden shower—
>> and I am riding naked
>>> on a naked horse.

manages to suggest not only relief from heat, but also the feel and smell of wet horse.

There is some difference of opinion as to how long beginners should stick to the purely pictorial type of haiku, and even whether observations made with other senses should be allowed from the start. Our own opinion is that it depends on the individual. If it is natural for him to use senses other than sight, by all means use them. Even a wild fancy like Buson's

"fragrance-moon" haiku should be acceptable provided that it is really natural.

In any case, it seems agreed that the mastery of objective haiku is the first step. It teaches observation, the recognition of what is (or is not) important in any experience, at least the beginnings of the art of compression, and, above all, that a haiku is a record of some particular moment of experience or intuition.

Inadequate as it is, this is all we can suggest for beginners. We can only add the following suggestions for both beginners and others, made by practicing poets.

Suggestions for Beginners and Others

J. W. Hackett, who represents what may loosely be called the Bashô school, and who is the author of *Haiku Poetry* (Tokyo, Hokuseido Press, 1964), has this to say:

1. Life is the fount of the haiku experience. So take note of this present moment.
2. Remember that haiku is a poetry of everyday life, and that the commonplace is its province.
3. Contemplate natural objects closely . . . unseen wonders will reveal themselves.

4. Identify (interpenetrate) with your subject, whatever it may be: "That art Thou."
5. Reflect in solitude and quiet upon your notes of nature.
6. Do not forsake the Suchness of things—nature should be reflected just as it is.
7. Express your experience in syntax natural to English. Don't write everything in the Japanese 5,7,5 form, since in English this often causes padding and contrivance.
8. Try to write in 3 lines, of approximately 17 syllables.
9. Use only common language.
10. Suggest, but make sure you give the reader enough, for the haiku that confuses, fails.
11. Mention season when possible, as this adds dimensions. Remember that season can be implied by the poem's subjects and modifiers.
12. Never use obscure allusions: haiku are intuitive, not intellectual.
13. Don't overlook humor, but avoid mere wit.
14. Rhyme and other poetic devices should never be so obvious that they detract from the content.
15. Lifefulness, not beauty, is the real quality of haiku.
16. Never sacrifice the clarity of your intuition to artifice: word choice should be governed by meaning.
17. Read each verse aloud, for unseen contrivance is usually heard.
18. Bear in mind Thoreau's advice to "simplify! simplify! simplify!"

19. Stay with each verse until it renders exactly what you wish to convey.
20. Remember R. H. Blyth's admonition that haiku is a finger pointing at the moon, and if the hand is bejeweled, we no longer see that to which it points.

He adds, as his own credo about haiku:

> There are values inherent in haiku which make it more than just a form of poetry. Prior to Bashô, the writing of great contribution to bring haiku to life by *basing* it upon intuitive (i.e. immediate) experience. Certainly haiku's real treasure is its touchstone of the present. As Bashô said, 'Haiku is simply what is happening in this place, at this moment.' There are, of course, important considerations involved in the expression of haiku. It is, however, the essence of haiku—the immediate life experience—which provides the real basis for its universal adaptation.

Advice, not necessarily conflicting, but with definitely different emphasis, is given by other American poets. Some of them, like Buson, stress the poetic, rather than the spiritual values of haiku. (These values are of course not incompatible.) These also usually advocate the use of imagined scenes as well as actual ones. In support of their position they refer to such poems as Issa's "dewdrop" (p. 50). In this, they say, the loss of his baby was Issa's actual experience; he simply could not have actually watched a real dewdrop "fade away."

Nicholas Virgilio, an outstanding spokesman for such poets, has sent in the following "Suggestions for Beginners":

1. Always carry a notebook. Jot down notes on natural phenomena . . . human and non-human: experiences, things, plants, animals—anything that strikes you poetically, or simply interests you.
2. Compose everyday:
   (a) Construct a word sketch, with respect to pictorial perspective; whenever possible place the most prominent object first; always try to present a clear picture.
   (b) With real and imagined experience as raw material utilize all your powers: fancy, imagination, logic, intuition, memory, etc.
   (c) Experiment: use a new or borrowed technique in all possible ways, with all manner of material and experience until your own style comes into the fore. Remember, even originality is relative; you build on what has gone before you.

We cannot here take sides between these two schools of writing haiku in English. We may, however, quote the words of Masaoka Shiki (both poet and critic, and a proponent of the Buson school), who said to those who had passed the beginning stage but were not yet masters: "Use both imaginary pictures and real ones, but prefer the real ones. If you use imaginary pictures, you can get both good and bad haiku, but the good ones will be very rare."

Dr. Tadao Ichiki, who taught haiku at the college level in America, suggests that two points should be gone into more fully. One is the development of a haiku from the first impression to the final form. He instances as an example Bashô's:

Shizukasa ya iwa ni shimiiru semi-no-koe

> This quietness:
>> the shrilling of cicadas
>>> stabs into the rocks.

or, in an attempt to keep the original order:

> So still . . .
>> into the rocks it pierces,
>>> the cicada-shrill.

The translation is inadequate, as *shizukasa* means also "stillness," "peacefulness," etc. But that is not the point. The point Dr. Ichiki makes is that in Japanese the first version of the haiku, which he calls "a mere report of the atmosphere," has no word in common with the final form except *semi-no-koe* (cicada-voices).

In the original version the first line was *yamadera ya* (mountain-temple); the "rocks" were "stones," and the verb suggested that they were "stained" or "dyed," rather than "pierced into." In a subsequent

version the first line became *sabishisa ya* (loneliness, or solitude). Ichiki notes that in this version "The solitary atmosphere is too strong . . . so Bashô changed it." In the final form Bashô was able to express exactly what he had felt.

The second point that Dr. Ichiki wishes to stress is that "The essence of haiku is suggestive brevity." This often requires the omission of words which can be obviously understood. And on this point he notes that "ellipsis is an important element of haiku. The pause or the gap involved in haiku may perhaps be likened to $(+)$ and $(-)$ in electricity, separated by a gap. The 'spark' jumps the gap between two apparently different or unrelated ideas, and makes a connection. The mind must make a leap."

In an elementary treatise such as this there seems little more that we can suggest to poets, except to emphasize the need for constant experiment. The Japanese haiku has traditions, standards, and conventions that have developed through the centuries. These, owing to differences in language and culture, cannot be taken over in two. Our poets have the task of developing traditions, standards, and presumably conventions of our own.

Experiment is needed, not only in form and in manner of presentation, but also in subject-matter

itself. E.g., can we use season-words? If so, how far? If not, what can we substitute to give an equal sense of depth? What limits should we give to the dictum that some aspect of nature is an integral part of a haiku? Do or do not Bashô's "white-haired family" or Bennett's "dusty tricycle" have sufficient relation to all nature to be haiku, even if the particular season is not recognized? Etc., etc., etc.

Experiment is needed in modes of presentation, particularly in haiku that are not primarily pictures. Also, a haiku, which is a poem, must sound like a poem, or it loses its effect. The Japanese 5–7–5 duration-count automatically gives a haiku a special rhythm and cadence, especially marked in the final line. This is not automatic in the English 5–7–5 syllable-count, unless we use only short syllables without massed consonants.

Experiment is needed in all kinds of devices, such as assonance, alliteration, internal rhyme, etc. Here the great danger is that of making the poem too beautiful, so that the words get between us and "the thing."

The basic objective of poets who write haiku in English is the same as that of poets who write in Japanese. They wish to let their readers experience, for themselves, the same living emotions that they

have themselves experienced. It cannot be done quite in the Japanese way; therefore it has to be done in our own way. It is a noble objective, and a great challenge.

Appendix

On the Reading of Haiku, Especially in Translation

There are so many different kinds of Japanese haiku poets, so many different kinds of emotions expressed and methods of expressing them, that for those who want to learn how to write haiku in English there can be no adequate substitute for reading as many Japanese haiku as possible. As W. H. Auden puts it:

> All one can do, it seems to me, is to give students as wide a variety of translated Japanese haiku as possible till they acquire an understanding of how the mind of a Japanese haiku-poet works. Then, of course, a gifted student may find . . . that the form can be adapted to one's own kind of sensibility. In the history of literature it is extraordinary how profitable misunderstanding of poems in foreign languages has been.

This is, of course, true. There is a real sense in which the Japanese mind differs from the American mind, or that of any other country. With different history, traditions, etc., it is bound to do so. And unless we do have some understanding of this mind it is impossible to grasp what a haiku is to a Japanese.

It is also true that a study of haiku written in

English already shows some adaptations which may prove viable. Others, however, are so far adapted that even though they may be poems, they are certainly not haiku. As G. K. Chesterton said, in speaking of freedom in the arts, it is a fine thing, but "if you feel free to draw a camel without his hump, you may find that you are not free to draw a camel."

One word of warning, however, may be useful to those who cannot read Japanese haiku in the original. It is this: "If, in reading translations, you come across a haiku that does not convey to you any emotion at all, do not blame yourself or the poet. Blame it on the translator!"

No translation of haiku is absolutely perfect. Many are incredibly bad. This is not only due to the difficulty of keeping, in translation, all the suggestiveness of a good haiku. Much of it is due to plain ignorance or carelessness.

A classic example of a printed mistranslation is that of Ryôto's (1660–1717):

Sore mo ô kore mo ô kesa no haru.

This is a sort of shout of joy at the coming of spring. (Literally: This too is all right; that too is all right! This morning's spring!) Not knowing that *kesa no haru* is a reference to New Year's Day, and confusing

the character for *ô* with the character *gan* (wild geese), it was once rendered as:

> A clear spring morning sky,
> And here and there, far overhead,
> Singing the wild geese fly.

This is an early example. But even modern translations, though not quite so flagrant, may be almost equally misleading. It is, indeed, quite upsetting to haiku to have Issa's:

> *Yare utsu na hae ga te wo suru ashi wo suru*

which is, as literally as possible:

> Don't swat it!
> the fly is wringing his hands . . .
> he's wringing his feet.

turned into a verse about not swatting "unhappy flies forever wringing their thin hands," which retains none of the humor, observation, and immediacy of the original and does not even mention the pleading feet, or to have Bashô's poem about the shrilling of cicadas piercing into the rocks (quoted on p. 64) given as "The crickets' singing's muffled by hot rocks" etc., etc. It is even more upsetting to find such verse being used by teachers as models for haiku in English

These two last examples appeared in publications, that, to do them justice, made no pretence to scholarship. But even in a quite recent book, with an important list of sponsors, both Japanese and Western, Buson's:

Hana chirite ko-no-ma-no tera to narinikeri

was given as:

> Cherry-blossoms having fallen
>> a temple stands
>>> among the leafy trees.

It does not seem possible to get from this any particular emotion, or even a clear picture of what Buson is seeing. Even a rough literal translation would have been less misleading:

> Cherry-bloom falling
>> a tree-interval (or between-trees) temple
>>> (it) has turned into.

Neither "leafy" (which gives a totally wrong impression of the scene), nor "stands" (which suggests a contrast with "falling") occurs in the original. Even worse, the statement that the cherry-bloom "has turned into a temple" has been omitted. The poem could be put into English verse in some such way as:

Cherry-bloom has gone—
a temple in among the trees
is what it has become.

Here one can at least get the picture. Where, only a short time ago, one could see nothing but cherry-blossoms, one now sees a temple—and precisely because the trees are *not yet* leafy. (When cherry-bloom falls, the leaves are just barely beginning.) This particular translation does not preserve the overtones of the original—the sense of gradual transformation, the suggestion that the blossoms are the *real* temple, etc., but at least it is not completely misleading.

The above warning is not against reading translations. They are all most of us have to go on, and most translations do preserve at least part of the emotion in the originals. But it is a warning against taking any translations—even those given here—as 100 per cent accurate.

In conclusion, the following suggestions to readers may be useful:

1. Remember that a haiku is concerned with one moment, and the emotion of that moment.

2. A haiku allows you to put yourself in the poet's place, and so to experience for yourself the circumstances that aroused his emotion.

3. A haiku is so short that it has to suggest more than it actually states. Hence the reader must consciously cooperate with the poet.

4. In a good haiku every word is important. The reader must therefore consider all implications including the internal comparison technique originated by Bashô as well as surface values.

5. Look for the season-word if it is there (as it usually is); it is an essential part of the haiku.

6. In a haiku of the objective type, it is vital to get the picture clear—before going on to any of its implications.

7. If, after proper study, a verse does not clearly convey the circumstances and/or the emotion involved, it is not a haiku.

8. Translated haiku can only very seldom convey the full force of the originals.

9. If a translated haiku seems not to conform to any of the four "general rules" referred to in Part 1, it is probably the translator's fault. "Forget it!" is usually the best advice possible.

0. Sometimes a trained haiku reader can experience

the force of the original Japanese through a mistranslation. This is worth trying.

11. A number of mistranslations are due to the fact that the same form of Japanese word may stand for both plural and singular. E.g., Kyoroku's (1655–1714):

Ichiban ni kagashi wo taosu nowaki kana

has been translated as:

First of all,
   it's scarecrows they blow down—
      storm-winds of fall.

A trained reader, knowing that no haiku is a generalization, would realize that Kyoroku must be referring to one particular scarecrow, and one particular storm, and the plural form should not have been used.

12. A reader must be prepared to do some work on any haiku, even if it is no more than visualizing a picture. On many (possibly most) translated haiku it may be necessary to do work over and above the normal call of duty.

Other TUT BOOKS available:

Please order from your bookstore or write directly to:

CHARLES E. TUTTLE CO., INC.
Suido 1-chome, 2–6, Bunkyo-ku, Tokyo 112

or:

CHARLES E. TUTTLE CO., INC.
Rutland, Vermont 05701 U.S.A.